God's
Will
for

Monsters

God's Will for Monsters

Copyright 2017 by Rachelle Cruz

ISBN: 978-0-9970932-4-7

All rights reserved

Cover art "Where My Mother's Breath Perches" by Trinidad Escobar

Figure photos used under Creative Commons License. Original photo by
    Philbert Charles Berjeau is now in the public domain.

Author photograph by Julia Ainley

Book design and layout by Lawrence Eby

Printed and bound in the United States

Distributed by Ingram

Published by Inlandia Institute

Riverside, California

www.inlandiainstitute.org

First Edition

God's Will for Monsters

Rachelle Cruz

Contents

Introduction

Rachelle Cruz's debut collection, *God's Will for Monsters*, is beyond ready to burst itself open, and bleed.

I first came to know of Rachelle Cruz a number of years ago in the Mission District of San Francisco. She read poems at a Kearny Street Workshop event at Litcrawl, and she impressed me with poems, finely crafted, concrete, imagistic, and taut, narrative and personal.

I am always on the lookout for new Pinay poetic talent, young poets who find themselves on my radar precisely because they are at the right place, at the right time, doing exactly what they are best at. Indeed, this is what I blogged about her on October 13, 2008:

> I am glad to have attended the KSW reading at the Casanova Lounge on Valencia Street, an event we would have attended anyway, in support of KSW. Still, the reason why I am happy about the KSW reading is because I am so glad to have heard Rachelle Cruz read. I'd never heard of her before. Her bio tells us she has just returned to the Bay Area after a few years of studying in New York.
>
> I believe Cruz's work was the strongest of all the KSW poetic work at Litquake, for its very clean and rigorous uses of poetic form and line, concrete words and images, and specificity of objects and place. She told us she has an obsession with the aswang, the Philippine mythological creature who splits her body in two. The aswang is female, typically beautiful. Her top half flies

off into the night, and with her long tongue, she sucks the unborn babies out of mothers' wombs. Fascinating, scary stuff, and for poets and artists, the figurative female cleaving in two is too rich to pass up. Cruz wonders what would happen to the aswang if she were to come to America. And with Cruz, whose well structured litany is rife with very precise pronoun usage (they, we, you), the relationships drawn here are so interesting.

As well, Cruz handles modern urban myth in the form of the neighborhood fire hydrant, and her poetic speaker's expectations as a new New York resident. I can't emphasize enough her use of located, specific, and concrete, such that we see both the myth actualized, and that we see the poetic speaker as astute witness become a part of this scene/world. I noticed Cruz was reading from a chapbook. Afterward, I did buy one. It's entitled *Honey May Soon Run Out*, and I see it is a book of odes, Neruda-esque odes to things often taken for granted. Odes to times and events and phenomena we take for granted. This is a poet I really hope to see more from, and as well, this is a poet I hope to include in my future publishing projects and reading series planning.

What more compliments can I pay Rachelle Cruz at this point, except that to say that eight years later, I am proud to report I have been able to include her in so many of my Pinay-specific literary projects, and in the process, have witnessed this young Pinay poet's work grow in depth and complexity, never losing the crisp and concrete qualities that drew me to her work in the first place.

Some additional thoughts on the aswang, who has been historically, mythologically, anthropologically white-splained and man-splained back to us, the keepers of aswang story. She was featured in an episode of NBC's *Grimm*; her first appearance was of a dark, tree-climbing, wall-scaling ghoul whose *tik-tik-tik-tik* shook me off my couch, screaming and shivering. There, she was an ill-intentioned Filipina mother-in-law, plotting to devour her own grandchild from the womb of her Filipina American daughter-in-law, in order to prolong her own life.

And so in American popular culture, the aswang has made her brief appearance as a taker of life, but with little of the nuance and contradiction which make this creature so interesting to us American Pinay authors. Lynda Barry's aswang in *One! Hundred! Demons!* has also traversed generations and continents, affecting the weight and ambivalence of intergenerational Filipina relationships and trauma. Barry's aswang is mythic because she is intangible but ever-present. She is both the monstrous, perpetually angry mother, and the over-strained relationship between mothers and daughters. My own aswang, in *To Love as Aswang*, speaks to the emotionally and literally broken Pinay womanbody, fighting and sometimes dying for an opportunity to speak for herself.

Cruz's aswang embodies those nuances and contradictions; she exists in catalogues, marginalia, omissions, and footnotes, in litanies and prayers, in remittances to family "back home," in the hyperreality of American suburbia (the aptly named Whitman Street in Hayward, California), in the secrets women keep among themselves, and in the much honored tradition of tsismis, a social mechanism which serves to regulate the thought and behavior of girls, especially those whose bodies are on the cusp of becoming women.

This girlhood is rife with the perversity and cruelty—think of little Catholic girls veiled in white purity dresses, primed to become little wives—but these are seething just beneath the fine film of gendered gentility and civility, a thin veneer of the proper. The aswang's story, the one Cruz's poetic "I" and "we" are making, allows her the freedom to imagine her own possibilities, which she crafts (reconstructs? repurposes?) from the simultaneous expectations of chastity and childbearing, even if she must make these stories in whispers: "To tell you / the truth, / we hatch / story. / Words licked over / and wet, / flying, / ear to ear, / special delivery."

This is what Cruz's poems tell me: If you want to know what we are, we are the writers of our own contradictory myths and narratives, for all our defiance and impatience. For all our curiosity and mischief. For all our faith, our gothic religion. For all our vexing, imeldific beauty, for all our rebellion and familial responsibility. Savor these poems, suck the marrow from their bones. These are lovely, complex poems, "sweet and bitter as a plum," a braised heart, blood-warmed and wet.

Barbara Jane Reyes
Oakland, CA
December 2016

For Mamay

How to Open

I opened "Anorexic bitch" and found confessional lattice.

I opened confessional lattice and found hunger.

I opened hunger and found a reed basket.

I opened a reed basket and found emptiness.

I opened emptiness and found my grandmother.

I opened my grandmother and found my tongue.

I opened my tongue and found hot sauce packets.

I opened hot sauce packets and found "You pig."

I opened "Pig" and found my mother's girdle.

I opened my mother's girdle and found sweat.

I opened the sweat and found high heels.

I opened high heels and found a sugar bowl.

I opened the sugar bowl and inside my teeth.

I opened my teeth and found Lucas Chili lies.

I opened the lies and found a narrow tunnel.

I opened the narrow tunnel and found a fisherwoman.

I opened a fisherwoman and found St. Francis of Assisi.

I opened St. Francis of Assisi and found too many birds.

I opened the birds and found a nest of prayers.

I opened the nest of prayers and found millions of mouths.

I opened the mouths and decided to listen.

In tracing the linguistic annihilation of the priestess:

anitera

anitero

asog

bayog

bayoguin

bruja

bruha

bailan

baylana

bailana

babaylana

babailanas

catalonan

catalona

hag

hechicera

hecheheros

katalonan

maganito

whore

The root word - talon, meaning forest. Talons, she's sharpening her talons. Spanish readership of missionaries' accounts grouped the above terms as simply priestess / priest.

Brewer writes "it is important to note at this point that, unlike Spanish, the indigenous languages of the Philippines have neither gendered pronouns, nor suffixes to denote sex." The institution of gendering.

Some women I meet are not constrained by discursive conventions. Their transgression allows them to conceptualize femaleness with the priestly function.

Some men I meet are not constrained by discursive conventions. Their transgression allows them to conceptualize femaleness with the priestly function.

This is the *talon* where my mother's breath perches. This is how I praised my mother *anita*. The subjects are fond of tsimis and rearranging fried pusit on the platter. The subjects are fond of prayer and Sharon Cuneta's early cinematic career. The subjects are fond of renewing their InterLibrary Loans and Nicki Minaj's long growl. The subjects are fond of salted garlic peanuts, a breath to terrify monsters. The subjects are fond of checking their own pulses then listening for the witches who refused to burn.

What We Did With The Aswang

Hayward, California

At night, mother smudges our foreheads with ginger and steam. Her
song is a braid of witches who lift windows with a single, crooked finger
to slip inside and feed. Out of the fish-licked sky, home, a flash of tongue.
Outside, the tetherball goes slack and swings on the pole. No tree-houses
inside the damp hearts of Redwoods to whisper, *we're home.* Later, our
mother says, *no, not me, where did you hear that story?* We reach for the
fall of her hair, the split end we want to peel. We want to twirl the strands
between our fingers and start a vortex, a hole vacuuming us in, a planet to
story our own.

Foreword

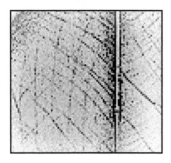

Figure 1

the Aswang,

    We acquired a live subject from a remote village in the province
  of Bikol
after fifteen years of fieldwork

contained for a week at the University   substantial interviews with
       comparisons to the European ordering of mythological creatures

many, elusive forms that the creature takes.   will further ease the
   reader's understanding

muddled

shape-shifting abilities;   from rabid weredog, to self-segmenting devourer.
not comfortable in a singular form.

    five manifestations:

Witch

Manananggal

Vampira

Weredog

Carrion-Eating Ghoul

> *Theories posit the Aswang's particular thirst*
> *which feeds the life source*
> > *bears the most resemblance to a witch, or bruja,*
> *who assists women with*

> > *refer back to Lilith (first wife of Adam), found in the*
> *Babylonian Talmud*
> *whose seemingly insignificant appearance birthed a tree of temptation*
> > *a tree*

Calling All
of the Aswangs of the World!

Calling:

late night victims, feminine wasters, thick-nosed words, rosary spill, toxic
cherry pop, studio portrait hymens, Fridas grown on fire escapes, bad
jasmine, big-tooth islands, blood lies, private-school panties, scrubbed
away tomboys, Planned Parenthood Liars for Life, bruised counselors,
camped knees, rice daughters, spoiled prayers, garbage disposal goths, girl
eaters, calamansi between fingers, shit talkers, jackfruit thieves, jam baby
jars, paper doll devourers, baby chewers, mint spitters.

you bitchy tadpole, pick up the phone, we've texted and called you, like
five times already.

An excerpt from:

1.) The Vindictive Witch

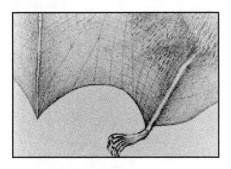

Figure 2

witch disguises

striking

    the role dutiful   vindictive

shopping at the marketplace, cleaning house and peeling roots,

               insert

objects

          seashells, rice, bone, pebbles

seeds into   her unsuspecting

    witch takes a deep breath and dives

(sst)

*

....

* Near death dusk
we conceive
a story.
A woman
with a flirty flapping
between her legs.
Her child
tries on her wings,
curly, or straight,
overbearing, or angelic.
Perhaps,
perhaps we
conceive women
with halos, lies,
black pearls,
wagging chins.
To tell you the truth,
we hatch
story.
Words licked over
and wet,
flying,
ear to ear,
special delivery.

How We Tried to Levitate

Hayward, California

In a circle
on the dying front lawn,
we slip our fingers
under our baby sister
and chant
light as a feather,
stiff as a board.
Flakes of ash fall from the hills,
smearing our foreheads.

Blades of yellow
grass in our sister's hair.
Her closed, ash-lit eyes
are two bowls of water
collecting rain.
Her body not stiff
enough to float.

It's the end of summer.
We smell plums
crushed into wet dirt,
their stones gnaw
into the backyard.

Streetlamps above us flicker,
while a neighbor girl
continues to chant,
somewhere
in the hills,
a house begins to burn.

The Girl Became

after Russell Edson

A woman had a daughter who was a stapler.
Stop gritting your teeth, girl. We'll have to stand
in line at the dental school, said the mother.
You'll miss school for a week. The girl coughed,
mashing her teeth and making a sound that
pricked her mother's finger. *I'm just trying*
to hold it together, the girl said. The mother glared,
bringing torn finger to mouth. The girl bit
the inside of her cheek then became a hanger,

and on laundry day, the mother would misplace
the girl, leaving her in a pile of hangers on the bed.
The girl's tongue creaked with rust. After the last
dry cycle, silence. The girl content enough to breathe
steam from her mother's freshly-pressed skirt,
the alumni sweater she often wore to bed.   Then the girl

squinted her smallness: a keychain. *Good! I've always wanted*
to get out of here, the mother said. The mother jangled the girl
into the ignition. *But this'll only take me so far*, the mother said,
while the girl forced the sun to beat brighter, ALOHA
FROM MAUI! her coconut bra knocking against the plastic frame.
Then the girl became the windshield, staring into her mother's eyes

fixed on the flashing dotted lines on the road. She knew what little came between her mother and the dark highway stretching west.

An excerpt from:

2.) The Manananggal

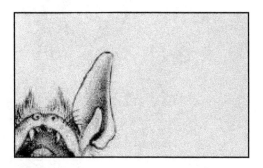

Figure 3

pre-dawn

shaded, unpopulated banana groves   she occupies

 to hide   shielded   creature severs its body

   in half,

                    protect   static legs underneath the wide leaves

        homes of prey: unsuspecting pregnant women.

searches for structural vulnerabilities in the prey's home, or for sheer

   neglect,

an open window.

                                        long, proboscis into

                                                and detach

What We Broke

Hayward, California

It began with a nick
from the crown of thorns.

Then our fingers brimmed
with blue paint and

his invisible left eye
lay broken in our palms.

In our parents' bedroom,
the statue stood between

two mirrors over
the wooden veneer drawers,

his hands heavy with air.
Every day, after school,

a scratch from
his callused feet, a comb

of fingers over the grooves
of his hair.

We
couldn't explain

the rainbows of
dust

on our cheeks.
Even after our mother spanked us

the Slipper or the Belt?
we swiped tiny curls

from the sacred heart, burning.
We wanted to dig for the fire

that made the heart beat,
our hands open to the beauty
of ruin.

How We Received Communion

Hayward, California

Our cousin cuts the paper doll's towering beehive,
shaping the hairstyle taller, taller
until her scissors hover
at the edge.
She sharpens the fingers,
the precise thin waist.

The paper between her knuckles.
We cup both hands and wait
for the fall of corners
we receive like cracked
pieces of communion wafer,

and announce,
This is my body
and swallow
before our cousin snips the last heel
and spills the dolls onto our laps.

How to Marry God

Hayward, California

Instead of a lace veil, straw hats fixed with a flounce of white ribbon. Our mother encircled the brims with crowns of honeysuckle, already brown like our eyes and wilting. Summer hats meant for a widowed church lady who fans herself with offering-cards. Her spindly fingers grip the cardstock, leaving damp wrinkles. We weren't going to marry God like the other little girls, pristine behind their veils. We were going to nag at Him from a boiling stovetop, demanding that he eat, eat, eat.

How We Kept Secrets

Hayward, California

She visited a witch doctor
who made her chew guava leaves and breathe
her legs wide and shaking.
We dream of her almost-baby, a fish--
swimming in a mason jar,
unscrew the lid with
the flat of our hands and dip our fingers,
splashing in the brine. The baby
snaps its jaw, pounds at us
with the force of her small, red body.
In the morning, we wake, gasping
aswang, our hands
cupping a small fin.

(sst):

*

....

*When we said "blame me," we really meant her.
When we said "melt," we stood here and didn't move.
When we said "pssh," we gathered together to pray.
When we said "bahala na," we pretended to knit and watch soap operas.
When we said "leave me alone!" we pressed our fingers against the peep hole.
When we said "drink," water dribbled from the corners of your mouth.
When we said "eat NOW," we busied ourselves with hot oil and dilis.
When we played music, the voice sang. always, always change.
When we pasted photographs into their albums,
we looked later for the smudge of our thumbprints.
When we texted "LOL," we really wanted to feel the heat of the real.

How to Kiss Christ's Feet

Hayward, California

Tonight is kissing wooden Christ's feet.
Tonight is songless, no numbers next to the altar,
no page numbers in dog-eared missalettes.

No sign of music except the 12 Stations,
like dance steps for a slow execution.
Auntie says to pray for forgiveness.

We suck in the heavy air, chap our lips.
An old lady in a black veil
five rows ahead drapes the crucifix,

a slung body, kisses the feet, and rests her
head there. On TV last night, men in the Philippines
were hammered to crosses on the shore,

zoom-in on their thorn crowns hugging
every curve and bump on their heads, and we want
to love that blood

as though it were coursing through our own lips.
See what they see in a plank of wood.

How to Fight Back

Hayward, California

The driver promises,
I'm gonna scratch up his car, pour
sugar in his gas tank and watch
the whole thing blow.
A girl inside a car of women, almost
women, speed down Mission Blvd to downtown Hayward.
Jalapeño poppers on their laps,
dinner. Miles away, their cousin cools her bruises
with weed choke, leaning on cold brick.
Motherfucker, the driver says, swerving past Whitman,
is gonna get it. Pipe and all.
The girl says nothing, sticks her hand out
of the window to cool a pepper.
Springtime red and dying on her face,
lilac fingers on her arms. She considers
spring a season for lovers, his smile, of course. She is convincing
with her hands. She hopes they are convinced. *Motherfucker,*
the girl repeats, burning her fingertips and lips on hot grease.
With more force and heat, she thinks, *this must be love.*

How We Became Filipina Youth of the Year

Back at the San Bruno Hilton Silver Ballroom,

sticking our heads in the steaming buffet trays

when no one is looking.

The picture in the paper—our hands breaking into a wave.

The Most Accomplished Filipina of the Year

is on our left in a conch-pink gown,

and the Filipina Sweetheart on our right

is in a rose A-line,

and all we can think of is Steel Magnolias,

my colors are blush and bashful, Julia Roberts

reaching out from the screen with her pouty teeth.

Glitter flutters from our strapless tubes

from Fashion Plaza, the one next to the Blockbuster

on Mission Blvd. Glitter sticks to our eyelashes, our mother's lip,

the photographer's lapel, the plate of lumpia.

When we were the Filipina Youth of the Year,

we didn't know what else to do but fill up

on stewed pork blood and rice

and watch the front of our dresses.

What else was there to do but memorize

"Phenomenal Woman" by Maya Angelou

and spell check our résumés?

(sst)

*

....

*Don't believe it. You were never
alone. Not frozen with a cold
locket pressed to your chest,
burning and orphaned.
Some picture of an abandoned
Anastasia in a newsie hat
with her hand
cupped out.
When you moved
through the kitchen
without speaking, you thought, silence
again? Silence a torch burning
the house, everyone
ignoring the smoke. You mixed
tamarind into sliced garlic
and stirred the water spinach,
the sweet-sour a fragrant prayer.
You always ate and drank juice
from the lip of the pan, a habit
we love, and you kept singing
burning your lips. This is the
silence we love, the moment
after you've slurped your last,
that salty breath.

An excerpt from:

3.) The Vampira

Once again, cannot resist the blood – the ultimate young men.

How to Vampira

Through the slurping of a straw. A cherry flavored Icee mixed in with blue cooler. A slow and steady slurp during midnight mass. Our hoodies cover the disco in our eyelashes.

The crack of knuckles when a man shadows his woman. The toss of a slinky dress. A woman pretending to not press the money into the fold of her bra. A woman yelling at another woman. A fistful of hair in her hands. We listen for the slam and crunch of glass chucked into the pavement. The sounds of quarters streaming through the lit-up jackpot machines with the numbers 777. We listen for the sound of malls closing and opening their doors, an ice rink producing the wreckage of snow and the blade against ice. Versace and Gucci and fur stoles. We like to hang out in arcades, casinos, where the light is never day.

Not just blood, but attention. We want the air to spike with fear, and the pressure of night to whistle like a kettle drowning out the house. We want glitter in their eyes for us. We want their bones to boogie. We want them to cross their legs.

Our Imelda Marcos

after Margaret Rhee and Susan Howe

O, Imelda Marcos, we wear your hair like a woven flag of sharp stars. We slip strands of it into our mouths, the ropey feel of abacá. Lou Diamond Philips is serving the clams again (he calls it "Cio-Filipino" and you deign to smile) and of course, you'd stir the sun out of their shells with a dainty oyster fork. The second best in San Francisco, you exclaim. Second best, you emphasize. Mmmhmm, we agree. Mmmhmm, blowing steam from your first spoonful.

As children, we collected seashells. On the shore and at the dinner table, scraping mussels' beards wet with our parents' slurp. Our father blew the dust from the metal-green shelf in the garage and laid out mesh for the shells to rest. He understood the beauty of corpses, the husks of them after we've eaten the living. And now, of course you are requesting another song, another dance. You're humming bailar la bamba when we're yelling Riiiitchie. Lou refuses to hum and sing, readjusting his chef's hat, tightening the apron around his waist. But he can't help it. Oh, Imeldaaaa, Oh, Imeldaaaa.

Beauty Triptych

> "I hate ugliness. You know I'm allergic to ugliness."
> —Imelda Marcos in the *Philippine Daily Inquirer*, August 1999

Beauty a gown with wings the color of butter melting in a frying pan. A perfect, steaming omelet slides onto plate.	Beauty a pair of rose pink kitten heels foxtrotting across Congress parquet. Meanwhile, a typhoon breaks open. A cotton dress shredded into pieces is good luck for someone else to sweep up and stitch back to life: a new school uniform, a blanket for the baby.	Beauty her satin-gloved hand tucked into Ferdie's. They wave at sun-spoiled faces in the crowd whose brittle hands scratch the sides of the stretch limousine. A gift of paint underneath their fingernails.

After Botticelli: Posing
as Imelda, Posing as Venus

We will be better
than Venus:
taut stomach,
swept-up dark-sugared hair,
Chanel-powdered face,
tits that peek through the cracks
of spread fingers.

Nipples disguised with rose
petals, of course.
There's still something
to be said about modesty.
Our chariot: a nautilus shell
plated with Yamashita's gold
(rightfully ours),
mother-of-pearl accents
the spiral outward.

Our daughters will toss
handfuls of sampaguita
for the camera's
signal.

We bite
our tongues
for the flood.
This is the flash
of light
preserving
our beauty.
This is when
we step out pure
from the ocean.

We Imelda Ocean

The ocean shatters each imprint on the shore, calling out mine, mine like hugging poker chips on the table with grimy arms, pulling them toward us, shaking our ha-ha-has, despite the unlucky hand of driftwood, ghost nets, six-pack rings. We lie when we say, We've loved them all, every bit.

Imelda Marcos untangles her headphone cords at SFO

and scrolls Artists 'M' Miles Davis *Kind of Blue* because she loves to
sing so what when the trumpet quakes. *So* what, so *what, so what. Okay
then, so what?* The blue from an Aquafina bottle sitting on the check-
in counter, half-drunk and still. Drops quiver below the cap when
planes hit the runway. The navy blue vest, crisply ironed, of the United
Airlines Attendant at customs who pressed her for an autograph. The
old kabibayan who left Manila before Aquino's assassination, before
Imelda reached the thousandth shoe, an Italian mule with a thick buckle.
Cataract blue rounding out the attendant's black eyes; ink from her pen—
staining Imelda's hand.

(sst)

*

*Here's the escape hatch for your mind / let your questions lie on the diving board / let them bake in the sun before jumping / into the clear pool / let your questions drink sugar water / from the patio feeder / let them dip their beaks for a few seconds while they flap their wings without stopping / here's the escape hatch / a cool drink of air / it's too warm out here we know / it wasn't supposed to be like this / but when we walked into the ocean this time / the second time / we didn't want to come back for air

What Cousin Taught Us
About The Body

San Jose, California

She says something about boys. We shake our heads no and think of crushes we could've had. Something about her barrio. We think a mud shack with an aluminum roof. Something about reglas. No, something about periods. No, we shake our heads, no. Twelve? We shake our heads again. Count eleven fingers. Eleven, a stuck out year. Something about breasts. She pinches the injury of our left bud and laughs. Something about permission, something about not allowing anyone to touch us there.

How to Deal with
the Problem of Evil

The problem with evil is—everything dark and shadow and your face disappearing. The problem with good is—virgin, virgin when all you want to do is stir your iced calamansi while ruffling that Björk swansuit on the cleft of your forehead.

There is a forest. There is an island of natives and your words are nothing but gentle coos. Not once, but twice, you called us "natives." Not once, but twice, you called yourself "native" and "anthropologist" and all of our houses stopped burning.

Litany for Silence

My mother in her flesh nightgown and I swallowed silence.
The bedroom door left ajar and I swallowed silence.
A book of refusal and I swallowed silence.
My sister's corded laughter and I swallowed silence.

Run home, run away, I swallowed silence.
The blacked out stars and I swallowed silence.
A book of strangers and I swallowed silence.
A man pressed down and I swallowed silence.

The elevator awaits and I swallowed silence.
Here, the lampshade of forgetting and I swallowed silence.
A book of good little girls and I swallowed silence.
My zipper ground down and I swallowed silence.

The gossip tree of women and I swallowed silence.
My darkening laughter and I swallowed silence.
Even at the forgiveness parade, I swallowed silence.
Wearing my mother's nightgown, I swallowed silence.

(sst)

*

....

* Look:
we measure
and soak
our fingers
in the rice water,
grains adjust inside
our fingernails.
Listen:
when we say,
we sat on his lap,
what we
really mean is.
Listen.

How to Prepare
Your Husband for Dinner

San Francisco, California

To braise a heart requires a kind of calm
about cruelty. She wrings out her tears
from a white kerchief, into a pot
that swayed above her head, whistling,
as if caught by a breeze. How the ears
will ease their burning after each fat
lie. How the eyes will steady their hungry
fire on her. No need for the briny bite
of fish sauce or shrimp paste; the tears
and shake of juniper berries are enough.
It's past midnight, and the water wails
on the stove. Husband will soon come home
stinking of hard work and damp dollars.
How close his bones softening in the broth.
Insatiable suck and chill of marrow. How he'll
stick, a piece of gristle she'll tongue for days.
How he'll sing between her teeth.

Tanduay, Motherland

In the cellar with the dead, the bones keep talking. They lift a finger to wag from the grave. In the cellar with the dead, my grandmother says, I refuse, I refuse, the flowers on her wrinkled duster growl.

Do you hear? This is my grandfather singing, Tanduay, Tanduay, cradling bonesharp bottles filled to the brim with sand. Motherland, motherland.

Here is the slow drip of the faucet. A dribble of water when he craved rum.

Even now, the air is wild from sugar fields. My mother bites down on cane, teeth gritted between sticky fibers. My grandmother sets a bowl down, shaking her head. My grandfather says, sugar, sugar, resting his arm on the kitchen table.

My mother fills empty bottles with peppered vinegar. The air is wild with sugared lace.

Their dreams hang above them, not the same dreams. My grandmother says, forget you.

Her children climb shelves and shelves for long rows of glass, their legs dangling.

A slap when the bottles hit the ground.

Why Flunking is Good for You

Hayward, California

We were sixteen, wearing fake, tortoise-shelled glasses and flunking out of confirmation class at St. Clement's. Slide after slide, the silky magma of a fetus. See, here's the baby, the teacher said. We squinted but all we could see were the red spurts from the inside of a volcano. When the teacher placed a salted fetus on her palm and called it life, we couldn't help but think of salted tamarind candy. (By the way, the rumors of old men squishing tamarind with their feet to form into candy didn't deter us from buying bagfuls from the market). The teacher's tongue shriveled like a slug on the pavement when we said had places to go, people to see. We walked home, over the train tracks, thinking about tipped Morton canisters, the girl trailing salt behind her.

An excerpt from:

4.) The Weredog

cause illness to those who look

in the snarl of its eye.

It is said that the pupils mimic a lizard startled in

sunshine

Calling All
the Aswangs of the World!?!

hey, we've written you twice. are you somewhere chewing strawberry gummies underneath the hem of some mother's cotton dress? yeah, us too. it's like camping in the attic with the humidifier on full blast. it's also kind of like threading hair from a brush into a friendship bracelet, picking lint from the teeth. is that creepy? yeah. remember that time you webbed your hand through our hair & the lake was full of twisted hangers? how every caught fish was a gift, you said, its guts thick as nutella.

MAXIMUM 25 WORDS

TRANSACTION	
Amount to be sent (in words)	Three Hundred U.S. Dollars
In figures	$300.00
Test Question	What is Girl's legal first name?
Answer	Girl.
Message	PLEASE RUSH THIS MESSAGE FOR YOUR NEW CANE MAKE YOUR WALK STEADY AGAIN OKAY? ALSO FOR MOM'S CHEMO DON'T FORGET
Signature:	

TRANSACTION	
Amount to be sent (in words)	Fifty U.S. Dollars
In figures	$50.00
Test Question	What did I study in college?
Answer	Accounting.
Message	FOR THE CATECHISM DRESS OF EDWIN'S DAUGHTER WHITE AND CRYSTAL BEADED PROMISE? FOR THE HOUSE ALSO TO HELP WITH FLOODING
Signature:	

TRANSACTION	
Amount to be sent (in words)	One Thousand U.S. Dollars
In figures	$1,000.00
Test Question	Where did we first meet?
Answer	Your wedding.
Message	DONT TELL ANYONE IM SENDING THIS TO YOU
Signature:	

In the tunnel between Montgomery and Powell Street, my mother says, *you know, we are underwater.* What, I ask, I can't hear you. My sister chews peppermint gum. My mother yawns a cartoon yawn. A pile of newspapers dance on the floor, I stop them with my heel.

TRANSACTION	
Amount to be sent (in words)	Twenty five U.S. Dollars
In figures	$25.00
Test Question	What's Mommy's favorite fruit?
Answer	Durian.
Message	FOR THE LACE CURTAINS IN THE LIVING ROOM AND THE WAX FOR THE FLOORS WHAT DOES IT LOOK LIKE?
Signature:	

TRANSACTION	
Amount to be sent (in words)	Two Hundred and Seventy Five U.S. Dollars.
In figures	$275.00
Test Question	What is your favorite ice cream flavor?
Answer	American cheese.
Message	FOR YOUR GEOMETRY BOOKS AND SWEET YAM AND RICE LUNCH AND SNACKS SHOULD BE ENOUGH STUDY HARD MAKE US PROUD OK?
Signature:	

TRANSACTION	
Amount to be sent (in words)	Eight Hundred and Fifty Dollars
In figures	$850.00
Test Question	Where did we first kiss?
Answer	At the movies.
Message	YOU BETTER NOT TELL ANYONE IM SENDING THIS TO YOU
Signature:	

In 2009, about US$17.348 billion in remittances was sent to the Philippines by overseas Filipinos, higher than in previous years. This is what Wikipedia says. I also learn that New Zealander Pinoys are called "KiwiPinos." Crossing the bridge, my father tells the joke about Daly City again.

TRANSACTION	
Amount to be sent (in words)	One Hundred and Fifty U.S. Dollars
In figures	$150.00
Test Question	What was my first dog's name?
Answer	Boy-Boy.
Message	ENCLOSED IS EXTRA FOR THE SURCHARGE DONT WORRY OK
Signature:	

Do you know why it's so foggy in Daly City?
Because all of the Filipinos are opening their rice cookers for dinner.

Why did the fog cook Filipinos?
Because they have the most self-es-steam.

How does a Filipino get a watermelon pregnant?
They pakwan.

How do Filipinos taste for dinner?
With their tongues, duh.

TRANSACTION	
Amount to be sent (in words)	Six Hundred U.S. Dollars
In figures	$600.00
Test Question	What is your favorite movie?
Answer	Flashdance.
Message	THIS IS FOR THE CEILING MONSOON SEASON AGAIN HUH DON'T WORRY THE RAIN WILL KEEP EVERYTHING CLEAN
Signature:	

The bronze bust of James Flood. My mother signs us into his building. Where she works. *He came looking for gold*, my mother says, *like me*. I try to stick my finger up his nose but there are no holes for air.

Ding.

The first door once the elevator opens. Black letters pressed into frosted glass: Odena Foreign Exchange. Tax. Remittance. Notary Republic. *This is why they call me the Jill of all trades*, my mother says. Tuloy Po Kayo. *Welcome.*

TRANSACTION	
Amount to be sent (in words)	Seventy Five U.S. Dollars
In figures	$75.00
Test Question	What's my favorite kind of music?
Answer	Disco.
Message	THIS IS FOR BLACK MADONNA LADY OF GOOD VOYAGE FOR INA WHO CROSSED THE RIVER
Signature:	

TRANSACTION	
Amount to be sent (in words)	Twenty U.S. Dollars
In figures	$20.00
Test Question	Where does Tita Cha-Cha live?
Answer	Germany.
Message	TODAY I FOUND A 20 DOLLAR BILL ON THE GROUND HERE WHO JUST LEAVES $20
Signature:	

I help my mother count the stacks of twenty-dollar bills wrapped in white remittance forms. Enough room for a small message from sender to receiver. Always this: *please rush.*

TRANSACTION	
Amount to be sent (in words)	Two Thousand U.S. Dollars
In figures	$2000.00
Test Question	What is my favorite Julia Roberts' movie?
Answer	Pretty Woman.
Message	THE LAST TIME OKAY?
Signature:	

TRANSACTION	
Amount to be sent (in words)	Fifty U.S. Dollars
In figures	$50.00
Test Question	What is Mommy's middle name?
Answer	Tiger.
Message	GOOD LUCK TO THE NEW BABY AND CONGRATS!
Signature:	

TRANSACTION	
Amount to be sent (in words)	Eight Hundred U.S. Dollars
In figures	$800.00
Test Question	What's my favorite home-cooked meal?
Answer	Number 2 at MacDo
Message	ENOUGH
Signature:	

A poster of a white sand beach fades into the background: Boracay. The coffeemaker drips done. Both flags gleam on Manong's camouflage hat. His fingernails brimming with dirt, telling a story of chess games, and canneries, white girlfriends, and SoMa.

On the train ride home, a woman dressed like a tulip sits in front of my mother. It is quiet, this goodbye to the city. My mother stares at the blonde hair in front of her. When the sidewalk descends again, the sun scatters through broken windows. She holds up a single strand to the light. The tulip turns around. *You had lint*, my mother tries to explain, tucking the hair into her coat pocket like a souvenir.

TRANSACTION	
Amount to be sent (in words)	Thirty U.S. Dollars
In figures	$30.00
Test Question	---
Answer	---
Message	DO YOU KNOW THE WINTER OF WORKDAYS MY PURSE CRUMBLING INSIDE THE HAND OF DAY FOR YOU ONLY YOU
Signature:	

An excerpt from:

5.) The Carrion-eating Ghoul

The creature's   cemetery   is satisfied   several weeks
hibernating   officers and Catholic priests   appear
archives. According to,

Salt and Holy Water   during   hunting hours,   killed
the precise moment of attack.

What We Learned from K., 1997

Baltimore, Maryland

We're not here. Inside the corner store, our best friend gazes at herself
in the surveillance mirror, braids and sleepy eyes, Disney's Goofy on her
hoodie, hiding the maxi-pads because she's afraid of what becoming a
woman might do to her. Now, her father speaks only to the space above
her head. The cashier pushes a pile of change across the counter, not
wanting to brush his hand against the shaking of her own. They're just
napkins, she says, explaining it more to herself. A box of twelve is lunch
money. Enough change for a pocket apple pie. Later, she will don a
beanie, sneak out of the apartment, past her father's television, to wrap
every bit of evidence in a ruined pair of underwear and deposit it into
the dumpster. Slink away like a criminal. If we could go back, we would
pollute every sidewalk crack on the way to school, past abandoned row
houses, at the drinking fountains at the mall, with perfectly wrapped,
pastel pink pads. At least then, she couldn't miss them, and she would
eat. No, we would hide them in mailboxes buried inside weekly
advertisements so her face wouldn't heat up from the shame. The shame
of her missing mother looking for God in bathroom stalls and 3 a.m. runs
for lake trout. If we could go back on a night like this, we would sneak
into the locker room, steal the instructional video, "What's a Period?" and
laugh our asses off, as if none of this was actually happening. We would
circle that dumpster like a pair of vultures, chuck every bit of ourselves
inside. Our howling and our cackling in the alleyway would echo the way
girls' voices do when they are not alone.

Neglect

"They went into my closets looking for skeletons, but thank God, all they found were shoes, beautiful shoes," Imelda Marcos told reporters when she inaugurated the shoe museum.

Sometimes we are heel gush and worn sole.

Sometimes we are termites engorging on Pierre Cardins.

Sometimes we are warped and stained.

Once we were the barong with the melting presidential seal.

Sometimes we are a sleeve nearly torn off.

Sometimes we are the battery-operated pair, blinking while she dances.

Sometimes we are unavailable for comment.

Sometimes we are donated at charity auctions, fetching ten thousand American dollars.

Sometimes we are the mosquitoes breeding outside of the Riverside Palace.

Sometimes we are tropical rains switching the channel.

Sometimes we are foil wrapped tightly around the antennae.

Sometimes we are the sopping cardboard boxes without return labels.

Sometimes we are scavengers licking dust from bone china.

Sometimes we are lighter than rain. Crueler than memory.

How to Teach New Monsters

Costa Mesa, California

The Deadline for Essay #3: On Monsters is the Monday after Spring
Break, after their easter eggs are boiled to crack, after they're dyed a
desperate pink of inside-cheek, after the vinegar lingers on fingertips
and keyboards. Now it's Sunday night, and our students are furious with
deadlines and in-text citations and block quotes, a few of their bodies
snap in half. Like pencils. Or aswang who sever torsos from legs, hiding
in mouldered banana leaves, the groves nodding their silence. During
attendance, one of them brags to another about wining and dining at
Planned Parenthood. Late again, this one braces her wings sticky from
flight and feeding, dazzling the whiteboard with blood. They hand
in their papers, and we're impressed. *What happened,* we ask. Before
sharpening her whistling proboscis, one of them whispers, *We learn only
from the best.*

How to Pray

Hayward, California

God loves you on your knees.
Prayers smudged onto the windshield aren't enough.
Tulip bulbs break from soil despite your waiting.
Your mother's mouth as sweet and bitter as a plum.

Prayers smudged onto the windshield aren't enough.
Her knees frozen on a bed of uncooked rice.
Your mother's mouth as sweet and bitter as a plum.
Your broken teeth fail you, now strung into a rosary.

Her knees frozen on a bed of uncooked rice.
Where you won't go: children inspecting stigmata on both feet.
Your broken teeth fail you, now strung into a rosary.
A thief leaves you stinging and penniless.

Where you won't go: children inspecting stigmata on both feet.
What is God's will for monsters anyway?
A thief leaves you stinging and penniless.
Every mother knows that.

What is God's will for monsters anyway?
Look: a heart drawn in Sharpie because here.

Every mother knows that.
You first saw glare but God in every window.

Look: a heart drawn in Sharpie because here.
Mystery is the pilot-light behind your navel.
You first saw glare but God in every window.
Humming theme songs and jingles, prayer.

Mystery is the pilot-light behind your navel.
Your mother's silence is good with your names.
Humming theme songs and jingles, prayer.
Beloved monster, nose pressed to the porch screen.

Your mother's silence is good with your names.
Tulip bulbs break from soil despite your waiting.
Beloved monster, nose pressed to the porch screen.
God loves you on your knees.

(sst)

We can't help but point to the beauty / this glass of water never runs out
so keep drinking / it wasn't your blood we wanted we just needed your
flames / listen listen / We can't help but whistle through our proboscis
some plain simple song about love / you know the one / We can't help but
crack the bone and suck the marrow / We were always taught to eat every
last bit / not a single grain of rice on the plate / We can't help but pinch
the air around roses / like you like us nothing can stop the unfolding of
light

Notes

"In tracing the linguistic annihilation of the priestess" riffs language from *Shamanism, Catholicism, and Gender Relations in Colonial Philippines, 1521-1685* by Carolyn Brewer.

"Foreword" and "An excerpt from" poems are inspired by *The Creatures of Lower Mythology* by Maximo D. Ramos.

About

Rachelle Cruz is from Hayward, California. She is the author of *God's Will for Monsters*, which won the 2016 Hillary Gravendyk Regional Poetry Prize (Inlandia, 2017), *Self-Portrait as Rumor and Blood* (Dancing Girl Press, 2012), and co-editor with Melissa Sipin of *Kuwento: Lost Things, an anthology of Philippine Myths* (Carayan Press, 2015). An Emerging Voices Fellow, a Kundiman Fellow and a VONA writer, she lives, writes and teaches in Southern California.

Acknowledgements

Thank you to Inlandia's Editor, Cati Porter, and the judges, rob mclennan and Meg Gravendyk-Estrella, for selecting this book. It's an honor to receive the Hillary Gravendyk Prize – she was an incredible poet who I admired deeply.

Thank you to Patrick Rosal, Brynn Saito, Juan Felipe Herrera, and Barbara Jane Reyes for their kind words. Thanks to Cherisse Nadal, Kenji Liu, Jenn Givhan, Éirann Lorsung, and BJR for their honest feedback on countless manuscript drafts.

Thank you to the editors at the following journals for publishing earlier versions of these poems: *TAYO Magazine, The Bakery, PANK Magazine, Splinter Generation, A Face to Meet Faces: An Anthology of Contemporary Persona Poetry.*

Thank you to the fellowships that have given me time and space to work on these poems: PEN Center USA, Kundiman, and VONA: Voices of Our Nation.

Thank you to my teachers, mentors and colleagues who've guided me throughout my writing process especially, TR Amsler, Jennifer French, Suzanne Gardinier, Tina Chang, Jeff McDaniel, Sylvia Sukop, John Boucher, Mehnaz Sahibzada, Erika Ayon, Thi Dao, Marissa Tinloy, Linda Brown, Bobby McCue, Chris Abani, Juan Felipe Herrera, Andrew Winer,

Goldberry Long, David Campos, Angel Garcia, Kamala Puligandla, Vickie Vertiz, Angela Peñaredondo, Ching-In Chen, Rachel McKibbens, Dan Lau, Sarah Gambito, Joseph Legaspi, Cathy Linh Che, Melissa Sipin, Edwin Lozada, Janice Sapiago, Mike Sonksen, Eddy Gana, Stephanie Sajor, Stephanie Hammer, and Kristy Bowen.

Thank you to the entire Creative Writing Department at the University of California, Riverside and the English Department at Orange Coast College. Thanks to Gary and Glynis Hoffman for their encouragement.

In gratitude for Gottawanna and DOTR for your unconditional love and example. Thank you for helping me find light in this book.

For Arielle, Kelly, Melissa, Rio, Yanni, Natalie, Jasmine, Andrea and Katie for their friendship and for showing up for me.

For the elders: Mamay, Papay, Lolo Judge, Lola Lourdes and Nanay.

Much love to my lovely and large family for attending readings, buying books, and always supporting my work: the Odenas, the Cruzes, the Lanuzas, the Dulces, the Morrises, the Alcalas, and the Albans.

For my sister, Jules, for reminding me to laugh and for her passion for social justice and education – you are a beautiful example to me. For my mom, Anita Cruz, for her generosity and love – for teaching me how to make books when I was a child. For my dad, Romeo Cruz for his insatiable appetite for writing poetry and open mics, and for always asking me, "have you been writing poems lately?" Thank you to my family for sharing their stories and for cheering me on always.

And of course, for Thomas, love.

CPSIA information can be obtained
at www.ICGtesting.com
Printed in the USA
LVHW09s0005160818
587148LV00002B/191/P